Heart Notes At Midnight

Tiffany Marin

Copyright © 2018 Tiffany Marin
T Mar Books
All rights reserved.

ISBN-13: **978-0692195536**

DEDICATION

To all of those who have inspired these pages,
I thank you.
To my children, follow your dreams!
Creating this book was one of mine.
To the Creator of all, thank you for the gift.

CONTENTS

1. First Love
2. Breathe In
3. The Meeting
4. Sudden Strings
5. Time Travel
6. Windy Be
7. Camp
8. Depths
9. Rest and Drizzle
10. Rise Up Lights
12. Fairytale
13. The Contract
14. Practice Makes Better
15. Above
16. Loved
17. Still Healing
18. Conversion
19. The Bittersweet Sting of Spring
20. Kindling
21. Portions
22. Concrete
23. Lovers End
24. Storm
25. Bond
26. The Island
27. Haiku – Blue
28. Faker
29. Whatever
30. Pout
31. Quietly
32. Wild Heart Rising
33. Clean Up
34. Sitting On My Bed
35. The Receiver
36. The Color Wheel
37. Once Missing
38. Shine
39. Dinner Date
40. Still
41. Container
42. The Chopper
43. On The Shore
44. Array
45. Mono
46. Blue Light
47. Inside Outside
48. Friday Night
49. Toolbox
50. Infinity
51. Waves
52. #9
53. Oxygen S.O.S.
54. Everything
55. Slightly Intoxicated
56. Words
57. Not Your Average Bear
58. Processing Pain
59. Sunrise
60. The Quill Express
61. Deliberate
62. Sigh
63. Truth
64. Transcendence
65. Man Down
66. I Heart
67. Fail
68. Gifts
69. Love
70. Go Time
71. Man
72. Taking Thoughts Captive
73. Open
74. Loving Myself
75. Experience
76. Kintsugi
77. The Call

First Love

Young, and in love
We were very much in love
There was nothing to figure out, it was obvious
It was free flowing
Open hearts
Full on
We were lucky

The heart gates wide open
So deep and magical
Being in love to that capacity
Was quite possibly a once in a lifetime thing
Though I hope the future will allow it to happen again

It all happened very quickly
A love like that is beyond words, really
We had what few experience
The timing was horrible
We needed time to grow
To learn
I wish we were able to see things then, as clearly as we do today

Our love is eternal
And sacred
Held in the highest regard
And always will be
Nothing will ever change that

There is a difference between loving someone
Being loved by someone
And being IN LOVE, together, simultaneously

It was the first real love for both of us
And we were in it 100%
It was special
It was ours
Without question
Indefinitely

Breathe In

Diving sometimes
Requires using your own air
Diving sometimes
Requires a tank full under pressure
Either way
You have to trust
That the air will sustain you
Dive fearlessly

Loving sometimes
Requires using your own air
Loving sometimes
Requires a tank full under pressure
Either way
You have to trust
That the air will sustain you
Love fearlessly

The Meeting

I know not of your personal ways
And you know not of mine
One day I hope to wake and find
That they have intertwined

We'll speak of our scars
And how we wished upon stars
And dreamed of big things to come

I'll tell you my stories
And you will laugh and smile
And say to me
"It's been a while"

I'm hoping that you will share something new
Finding peace and tranquility
A smile that reflects
Something more than just sex
An undeniable, indescribable curiosity

So let's have coffee
Start out as friends
I want to know you
And show you my spirit

Teach me to dance
We won't speak of romance
If we're quiet enough
We might hear it

Sudden Strings

Suddenly something
Suddenly there
Suddenly sunshine
Suddenly fair
Suddenly unexpected
Suddenly a whole new world
Suddenly floating upwards
Suddenly magically swirled
Suddenly changing the course
Suddenly so unsure
Suddenly abruptly ending
Suddenly different than before
Suddenly shocked and disbelieving
Suddenly in a daze
Suddenly shifting unwillingly
Suddenly something frays

Time Travel

It's a new day
Another day of silence
Keeping my peace
Allowing the distance
The days may as well be miles…
By now you're states away,
Claiming a new accent.
The miles may as well be years
As it's felt like decades in the hours that have passed
It's as if you never were sometimes
Truly a dream
I'll know with certainty when I see you again,
If this is real or a was then

Windy Be

Day three and I'm questioning my ability to read between the lines
Patience is what I need and to relax in Gods timing
I know what I felt...
Could feel my feet lifting as was my spirit
Now I'm a little lost in the whipping wind....
Eyes still on the ground where we were once found
I will see you soon and we will see
We will feel
And what will be, will be

Camp

Five days in the cold tundra
Barren
Quiet
Empty
The northern lights keeping me company
My own understanding of this place is not for me to grasp
Faith is my fire pit
And hope is my fleece-lined blanket
I don't want to be here
Unless, you show up with sticks & marshmallows
So, I'll keep the coffee on

Depths

I will not chase
I will not chase the world
As it runs away
I stand in my own gravity
Create my own reality
Aware of the chaos and insanity
Finding peace amidst the calamity

Stepping-stones
Heartbeat groans
I'd rather feel and reel
Than close down, dry up, and peel
The layers revealing
A molten center
Ever churning and burning
With a desire to share the heat

They say there is value in the intangible
And this is true
You cannot touch love
Yet love remains
It's value ever present
In the sunshine and the rainy days

Rest and Drizzle

I want to sleep tonight
After a day of sleeping in
Put the pen down slowly
And let the night seep in

Rise Up Lights

White, crumpled, warm sheets that hold the secrets of our passionate night
I'm lying in our love bed
Surrounded by his scent
My satisfied yet saddening body savoring every moment
As the time ticks down
And my lover is walking gravely away from me towards the door
The suitcase dragging against the carpet as if to say, no, do not go,
It is against the grain
His dewy soft eyes locked on mine, looking back at me
As I keep our nest heat alive for a little while longer
My arms outstretched towards him as if they could reach him,
Reaching, stretching, all the way to my fingertips
I call out his name
In a longing way
As if through a wind gust that carries my heart song with every letter
He stops at the door
Taking in one last long stare, fighting the inevitable
I know that he wants to be back in my arms
As they are still outstretched, begging for his return to them
I call out his name again, slowly, sleepily, raspy, deliberately
Our hearts still beating as one
Regretfully, he opens the door, eyes locked on eyes, and he whispers goodbye
We stay together, desperately wanting more time, holding on for every morsel as the door space slims to a sliver, and then to a close
My arms collapse
I hold his pillow to my chest and nuzzle my chin in
I wrap my arms around myself and embrace us, as he would have
A few slow tears lull me back to sleep
It would be the last time we saw each other

Continents separated us
Lives on opposite sides of the planet
A cosmic love that travelled across oceans
Would still be felt over the next year
We'd write each other
And have phone calls where sometimes we'd just breathe together
To share the same space again

It was the greatest and saddest love affair
And it all started with sand under my feet and sweet music in the air

Fairytale

Romeo, Adonis, Prince Eric
Your creation is a burden
To make me dream of a love like that

Consumed the poison
Attacked by the boar
Passion to the death
And the story left incomplete
Only to trail off into the improbable happily ever after

I am Capulet, Aphrodite, and little Ariel
Yet alive and dreaming
Star gazing
Heart sighing
Ink well

The Contract

Someone once said
Marriage should be a 10-year contract
Able to renew or release every 10 years
I never forgot that

"Forever" was stamped on the wedding favors to my guests
Forever, lasted 7 years

If there had been a contract
Maybe there would have been a way
A way to say, we've got 3 years to make this work…
What else can we do?

I did good with deadlines
So did you

It's just so sad
We couldn't make it through

You didn't see me for me
So apart we grew

I used to think that contract was a bad idea,
A not so good thing
But maybe it's not worse,
Than seeing my hand without my ring

Practice Makes Better

I'm hearing, let go, let go, let go.

I want to.

Trying to visualize what that looks like
So that I can

Three fingers on a string to the heart shaped balloon
Just open your fingers

Long stemmed scissors in my right hand
A braided cord in the other
Just snip

How else do you do it?

A scarred heart, my journals, a jumbled mess of tattered strings in a heap on top of a silver platter…

Handing it over to God on the throne
"Take this."

I suppose that is how

But the memories, the pictures, the history, the kids

I see them every day

Open fingers, cut the cord, serve the platter.
Repeat.

Above

An honest reflection
Whether honored or not
Is still honest and true
I will always look forward
While using the past as an example
To determine future steps

Nothing is concrete
Memories to serve as flexible indicators
Of how things may turn to replicate or
Morph themselves into anew
Perspective is everything
And best at a bird's eye view

To love is to let free and hold tight simultaneously
Personal truth never to be compromised
Or to allow others judgments to sink in
Honored by ones own thoughts of self love
Fly like an eagle
Grace like a dove

Loved

Someone asked me recently if I was doing alright or having a hard time.
The answer is both.
On the inside and the outside the picture is both.
The truth is both.
In the grand scheme of things, the bird's eye view perspective...
Is that I am doing better.
I've had better days; I've had much worse days.
The good outweighs the bad now.
The structure of the angles and dynamics are different, but the general consensus is better.
When I'm down, the weight is measurable by the extremity of pressure.
When I am up, there is little gravity to measure.
One frequency has stayed the same though...
To be loved and cherished as the bird that I am.
Not from a distance,
Not in partiality,
Not as the fair weather turns,
But with the deepest of complexity,
Into depths like the ocean,
To be handled with such great care as one would with the most delicate and fragile of gifts.
And so I wait.
Doing alright,
Having a hard time,
Doing better.

Still Healing

I don't really remember what it was like kissing you.
But I do remember the hugs.
The hugs I will hold onto.

Conversion

Plans are what we think we want
Plans are thoughts – best laid out
Nice and neat in a perfect world...
When all goes according to plan
Plans change
And they should when the shoe fits
Walking a line is easy enough when you can see it clearly
When rain smudges the line
And the oil slicks
And swirls and drips
Things get slippery
The line no longer a line
It's a colorful display of change...
Intertwining lines alive with depth and shine and messiness
It's been raining for a while now
Rain changes everything

The Bittersweet Sting of Spring

In the darkness of night
And in the delicate illumination of the bedside table lamp
In the shadows of the day
Within the pale light peeking through the vertical blinds
Under the shade of the overcast sky
Completely exposed to the passersby
Within the hours of soul exchanges via fingertips on the keyboards
As the messages ping across the electric screens
In the twinkle in your eye
And the sweetness of your face
When we smile at each other across the glossy public place
In the nonchalant hugs that tingle with desire
When we hope that no one is watching
In this space
In this time
You are my lover for all of time
You'll always live here for me
And I'll live here for you
When this borrowed time has come and gone
When life and loves embrace us separately
Know that this will always be ours
Forever, as lovers, indefinitely

Kindling

Free to explore this frequency
Released from the invulnerability
Slipping into this place with you
Is intoxicating, and I have yet to taste it

Fervidly awaiting your heat
Eager to let my love flow
With no hindrance or conscious protection
Fearless with anticipation of this energy

The time is near...
I can already feel you...
Now, my lover, feel ME.

Portions

My cup is full.
My plate is empty.
I am stuffed with satisfaction.
Thank you for filling me up,
And the second serving,
And dessert.

Concrete

So much love to give
It hurts.
That care I received though-
Wow, so amazing to be so considered.
I want that now for always
I will not settle for less
It is a new requirement.
Our connection...
Your words...
So pure, so sweet
The tenderness of your love is the best thing I've felt.
Heart melts...
Into a puddle on the floor

Lovers End

When you left,
I cried.
Saying goodbye, closing our time together,
Would be easy enough, I said to myself.
I lied.
Part of me walked out that door with you.

Storm

Trying desperately to fight the treasonous tears
Putting on my best acting face
I know I have control over my thoughts
And I did good for a little bit
But the recent sweet memories rage in like a flood
Hard not to drift into them
Refocusing my attention
Seemingly every few seconds
Only to be brought back to the undertow

Little white flag waving from my heart...
It's only been a day since we've been apart.

Bond

Love together
Cry together
Kiss, kiss, kiss

Hands together
Ache together
Kiss, kiss, kiss

Once together
Goodbye together
Miss, kiss, kiss

The Island

Months of loving on me
And yet, we are right back at the beginning
Keeping me at bay
Keeping yourself at a distance
Reaching out to touch me
When you need me
Pushing me away when it feels too good
Loving me in convenience

Swaying between my layers where air is not necessary because love fills the lungs
And back to shore, where you gasp for air
Unsure of how you were breathing with me
Fingers gripping the coarse sand
As you pull yourself out from my ocean
The twinkling night sky covering the pair of us
Feeling, feeling, having felt… what many may never

I hope to meet you again in the middle
Or close to the end
In the space where time and sand and air were secondary
Where the possibility of chartering these waters was a bright idea
Brighter than the dark fears of circumstance
Where love was the lighthouse
And together we were the island

Haiku – Blue

Bath water fading
Refilling reluctantly
With my salty tears

Faker

You took me to the cheese grater
You pushed me up & pushed me down
You peeled off layers of sensitive skin
You shredded me

And then you were happy to sprinkle my essence all over your soul food

Taking part of me
And claiming it to be you
Merely because you shredded it

Whatever

You're probably happy that it's over
Happy to have your heart freedom back

Meanwhile mine is squashed
I feel like shit
And I can't get anything done

You can avoid feelings
You know how to stuff them
Which is cowardly

But I cannot.

Go on
Enjoy your life
Like every other man who was not man enough
To love me the way I need to be loved

You don't cherish me…
Maybe only the memories

Lucky you.

<u>Pout</u>

I've grown tired of thinking of you
But I'm still growing
And still thinking
So... boo.

Quietly

I want to say, let me go…
I want you to say, I can't do that.

My heart wants to beat with yours.
Again.

Bodies mashed together, lovingly…
Eyes on eyes, seeing beyond the iris…
Into the vastness that is a soul's soul.

I want to say, stay…
I want you to say, I can do that.

Wild Heart Rising

A champion always rises
Daggers upon daggers in my heart, my side, and my back
But I will stand
For you to watch me bleed
One by one, I'll remove those weapons that were meant to harm me
I will keep my gaze on your eyes – as you watch me heal myself
I will want to throw those daggers back at you – but I won't
You have your own to use on yourself – my eyes will say to yours
I hope that you will lay your weapons down
Nobody should have to experience such agony – self inflicted or otherwise
Daggers, arrows, swords, & all other impaling tools for wound creation lay on the dusty ground at my feet
Surrounded by staining blood and piping hot tears
Pooling, drying, evaporating, rusting, disintegrating
As I stand regaining my strength, clarity, and focus
Preparing
Breathing
Shoulders back, head high
Hair blowing in the sun-kissed wind
I am a warrior
I am a champion
Undefeated
Breastplate & shield removed
I will again expose my heart
Unafraid
Unashamed
Beating harder, beaming brighter, stronger, wiser, larger
A much larger target now
Simple metals unable to penetrate this gold
Steady now
Steady now
I'm walking here
And the dust kicks up behind me

Clean up

I want to say goodbye
Lock safe and store away these heart feelings

Then I see you
And all these feeling boxes tumble off the shelf

Sitting On My Bed

Turn the music down in my mind
And listen to my heart
The silence is ringing in perfect pitch
My ears cannot hear my heart
Only that ringing
Slow the thoughts down, way down, turn that volume down
Break from the noise of the distractions
Take a deep breath
In, out,
In, out
I see the dawning of a sunrise in the distance of my mind
Eyes closed
I am calm.
This was not the case just moments ago, when all hell broke loose from my eyes and soaked the flesh of my face.
Replaying those sweet memories, yes, the sweetest ones
I lose myself in the beauty of those moments
Those moments of pure innocence, friendship, and lovers looks
It was all in the eyes, the tender touch, rooted in desire
And respect, and care, a mutual crossfire
The honesty of those fleeting moments never offering a clue to the mystery that is why we are here now, reminiscent of our past, feeling distant,
Having said farewell to the opportunity that love granted.
Oh that ringing silence!
You are not a comfort to my troubled heart.
And so, I allow the noise to crowd back in
To fill in the cracks of shattered dreams,
To distract me from the lovely things
That once made me so happy.
Neither the memories, the silence, nor the welcomed noise
Release me.
It's a tug of war that my mind and my heart cannot win.
Just breathing is my only option
And looking forward to that blessed sunrise.

The Receiver

Love is love
And there are those that use love to get what they want
There are those that live love in authenticity
There are those that want love
But are unable to receive it
Because it is unfamiliar territory
Love is at the center of who I am
I give love naturally
To withhold love would be an uphill effort
I use love to share love
To pour it, to feel it,
To sow it, to seed it
All I want is for someone to water me with it
Consistently
I want what I give
I give to give
I want someone to want to give it too

The Color Wheel

The crackling amber fire speaks to the intensity of my love-
A flame starting low that rises above,
That will engulf and dance and beg for romance.
A clear polar ice block, stacked into a cylindrical princess tower, with one side crumbled and tumbled, hollowed and scattered onto the ground below, shows the destruction and brokenness of something that was once so beautiful and bold.
Pale pink & coral with reflective lavender, bright soft satin, the delicate petals of a wild flower, that speaks of my soul.
Teal and turquoise and powdery blue swirl together to showcase my creative glue.
Charcoal and black are my coverings and shield to protect the royal plumb heart that shivers against the steel of a silver tongue-lashing.
Midnight blue with white stars flickering light, is to my imagination stretching through the galaxies as the color of night.
The jade green blade of a sliver of grass is my new nature arising from dark soil laid upon ash.
The yellow sun, burns it's rays of warmth, it brightens my path, shows my future set forth, the abundance of the aftermath.
There are so many more colors, more mixtures to explore...
I am all of the above, and then some, much more.

Once Missing

One day
Some day soon
A special someone will see me
And I will see them
And we'll no longer be in a bin
With other discarded or left behind items
We will finally be found

Shine

Too much exposure to the sun
Leaves a burn
And what of loving?
Both sun and sand and warm body
Exposed without protection from the rays
Breathing in the salty air
Ocean filled with telling tears
That battered shore where the water breaks itself
Rolls in then pulls away
Tiny bits of ancient shells glistening in the same light
It's all me
Every element
Especially the burn
Redness covers my skin
I cannot escape the heat
And with every gentle breeze that grazes me
Graces me
I drift softly
Ebbing with the tide
Watching
Waiting
Hoping
Loving anyway

Dinner Date

I paid the tip and got no kiss
Hard to gauge him in all of this
I'm tired now and want more sleep
So goodnight to myself
To myself I'll keep

Still

I still believe in love and romance
I still believe that there is a magical love out there
Being prepared for me
Just as I am prepared
To pour my love magic all over that someone

Container

Will any man let me love him full force?
If this gift has been given to me
There must be a purpose for it
Surely a man who is capable of receiving it is out there
And he is waiting for me
Maybe he just doesn't know it yet
When we meet, that intensity, that desire,
That heat will have a place to fully expand
I am ready to take the lid off

The Chopper

The spark of the writer can flicker bright in an instant
It can dim just as quickly
The midnight writer awakens just enough to pen her prose.
Eyes closed, fingers tapping on the keys
A hopeful sense of creativity
Not looking to change the world
But to be a spark that may ignite another
As the midnight writer rides
There's freedom from captivity
The nights are bright
The days are dark
There's magic in the fluidity
Come to me friends
Show your colors
Bring forth the best of me
The wind is whistling wistfully through my hair as the warm sun kisses my shoulders gently
I ride through the canyons, bandana soaking the sweat from my brow
The road is open and accepting of me
This is my valley of sun and sand
Peachy bedrock and mild glitter tones
And coyotes in the distance howling their song of marked territory
The dust kicks up behind me but I am looking ahead
The lone rider,
Midnight writer,
Riding,
Writing steadily.

On the Shore

I tossed and turned all night
The waves and wind of my mind still thrashing around a bit
I don't really know what direction I'm facing

Surely I did not make any decisions in the darkness of night

I merely sat in my boat, checking my gauges and instruments,
Trying to read them through the rain

I was holding onto the wheel, so as not to capsize
But allowing the waves to carry the vessel

Dawn is here and I'm feeling a little seasick

I want to have my feet on land, so I can regain my stability
Let the sun dry me off
Let my eyes refocus
So I can take inventory of my faculties

I know who I am, but this is new territory

And you are uncharted country

<u>Array</u>

I'm so tired... I want to sleep this away
Pretend it's a different day
And that you hadn't responded that way
That you DID want me to stay
And not let anyone else be in the sway
Because I am more than what they say
I'm worth more today
Than I was yesterday
Because I'm stronger in a way
In all my truths, in all my play
I want you to chase and fear not what may
Be different tomorrow or the next day
Because life is too short to push love away
Closing my eyes to pray
As the sky outside is gray
Tears will fall anyway
Goodnight, fare thee well, Namaste

Mono

It's safe to say that I miss you
This is why I needed space
To understand the feels in the heart place…

It's safe to say that we had a good thing
Things were almost as I would've liked them to be
So understand we couldn't feel to full capacity… free

It's safe to say that the universe is making a music track
Hearing songs that we enjoyed at every turn
Not understanding why that is necessary… the burn

It's safe to say that missing you may be good
And I hope that you are missing me too
And that you understand why I wanted it to be
Just you and me

Blue Light

I look at my phone hoping to see a message from you
But I know you won't send one
I keep looking
And hoping
And knowing better
Yes, I know better
I am better
Better than this

Inside Outside

Stop invading my thoughts right now!
No, don't stop.
I like thoughts of you.
Are you thinking of me?
How could you not be?
Sending you telepathic messages right now!
Hi! I miss you.
It's 6:35pm on Monday.
Two days after you walked away from us
Not so much as a chance to see
What we could be...
What it feels like to be a "you & me"

Friday Night

Surely you dropped your phone in the toilet
Surely you had a family emergency
Surely you took cold medicine and passed out
Surely you wouldn't say goodbye to me
Surely this thing, this whatever it is
Is more than whatever has distracted you?
Surely someone didn't catch you off guard
Surely this thing isn't over or through

Toolbox

I've become accustomed to heartache in a way...
It makes for good writing.
I am a writer.
I am all heart.
I am not broken.

<u>Infinity</u>

Our last kisses were under the stars
Our last embrace engulfed in the wind of night
Our last laugh set to music on the radio

The stars will last for lifetimes
The wind never dies, nor has a beginning or end
Laughter and music live on

As does my love for you

Waves

Thoughts of you are so distracting
My insides still a jumbled mess
Getting through my day only halfway present

The pit in my stomach still there
As it rolls in with the tides of anxiety
Waves that sometimes take my breath away

It's not fair to be suffering like this
I miss your face, your smile, your smooshy kiss

#9

Love sick
Body shakes
Butterfly belly
Mind quakes
Thoughts of you
Feeling sad
Full on love flu
I've got it bad
Waiting for
Open door
Open window
What's in store
Cure the ill
Make it well
I've had my fill
Of achy swell
You're the doc
I'm the nurse
Tick tick the clock
Makes it worse
Rest rest rest
Eyes closed and open
Who would've guessed?
You're my lovesick potion

Oxygen S.O.S.

Even the fresh air is suffocating
There is no place for me to cry at work
So I weep internally
Still so confused as to how this could be
I've handed this situation up to God
But my human body is still in mourning

Was it all a dream?
It felt so real
Unbridled happiness for 30 days
A sucker punch to the guts
The devil plays

I want to sleep until this passes
I'm all beat up about it
To lose what could have been
To have that ripped away
It's the unexpected and the unexplained
That has me caught up in this hurricane

Everything

I have nothing to lose
But in losing you
I lose everything

<u>Slightly Intoxicated</u>

I refuse to believe that what you said to me is your absolute truth...
I refuse to believe.
I'm going to trust in the space of time.
In the place where the truth is...
Where I am yours and you are mine.

Words

So I suppose you are a perfect person?
Never making mistakes?
Never saying the wrong thing?
Never making someone feel unwanted?

No.

You are not perfect.
You've made mistakes.
You've said the wrong thing.
You made me feel unwanted.

And despite your imperfections,
And setting aside my own transgressions,
My heart still speaks your name.

Together we'd never be perfect.
Perfection kills progress.
Forgiveness is the foundation.
Within risk is the reward.

Not Your Average Bear

Somebody must have hurt you pretty badly
Somebody must have bruised your heart
Somebody that you must have loved

Everybody goes through times of trials
Everybody goes through phases of rejection
Everybody has been wounded by someone who loved them

Anybody can tell you that I am different
Anybody who knows my heart can testify
Anybody in my life would be willing to share my story

Nobody would say that I operate outside of love
Nobody believes that I have less to give
Nobody who knows me

I am somebody who is not like everybody
And nobody in my circle thinks that you were just anybody

Processing Pain

So distraught, walking through the public places
Trying to keep myself in check
I'm so overwhelmed by your decision and how I made you feel
I am a lover, not an ultimatum giver
Such a poor choice of expression that I can never retract
And so my heart is shattered
And grieving this loss
I feel like I have been waiting for you my whole life
But now I am here, having fallen face first in to the pain pit
I am still stunned
Burdened by my own words
Tears chasing tears down my face
Complete disbelief that you have given up on me so quickly
I'm still going to pray
I'm still going to dream
I'm still going to hope
And wish upon stars
That you'll miss me
And come home

<u>Sunrise</u>

We could have been
Waking up in each other's embrace this morning
Feeling that sweet connection that is a rarity in life
I was looking forward to many mornings with you

We could have been

The Quill Express

It's been over 48 hours since my heart note was in your hands
My cursive swirly handwriting reaching your eyes
My true nature on debut on the smallest stage in the world,
right there, just with you
Amplified on paper

I hope you feel me there
Every time you read it
Every time you turn the page
Every time you close your eyes
I hope you hear my voice
And remember how you felt
When we were falling for each other

With hope, I'll wait
But not forever
My heart spilled out
Penned on love letter

Deliberate

Patience is not a virtue
Not when it comes to me and to you
I fidget and I pace
Back and forth
A heartbeat race
Something about your energy mixed up in my space

I'm usually calm and collected
Mindful of the words I use
Tactful in my delivery
Never fearing of something to lose
I am who I am
Mistakes, wrong steps and all
Subject to imperfection
Bound to miss and fall

The ball is in your court
You're the judge who will determine this fate
Truth is what you make of it
I hope it's not too late

Sigh

I just want to write about you...
And how you've affected me
Even if I feel silly one day
For falling apart inside this way
I don't regret it
It's probably nothing and I'm just getting carried away
Ok. It's okay.
I give myself grace.
I just want to write about you...
Write about you
Write about you
Write about you
You, you, you...
And me.

Truth

I am in love with you.
I fell at the same time that you did.
I am grateful for that night...
Liquid courage or not, you told me.
And I believed you.

Transcendence

Harnessing my energy towards you
Praying for a break through
Sending love thoughts and summons
On the light barriers
Travelling beyond this realm
In hopes of reaching your heartstrings
Faith the size of a mustard seed
Still carries the power of my infinite love
Earthly time having limitations and boundary
I wish to breath beyond that
To speak through the twinkling of stars
For the falling of rain to tap sweetly on your soul
For each drop to tip the scales of your indecision
For each passing moment to bring clarity and light to your heart
Remember us
Remember us
Harnessing my energy towards you
Praying for a break through

Man Down

When is enough, enough?
At what point is the pain bucket full?
It feels as though it's been overflowing already
Like it is still swelling, still throbbing, still inflamed
I don't know what I'm supposed to do
Exquisite memories of you
PTSD of the heart
I'm lying in an empty field unable to stand up.
Shot down in shock
Paralyzed by the shrapnel and its sting
Songs of hope and loss playing on loop over the loud speaker
Daytime, nighttime, in between dreamtime
The buzzing sign with your name on it
Flickering constantly
Enough to keep me awake
And also to greet me in the first thoughts of the morning
I want my life back
I want my heart stitched up
I want you to know how you've affected me
In the desert, in the flood, in the snow

I Heart

I don't like hurting this way
Feels like wasted time
I'd rather be loving

Fail

I really freaking miss you
I really really really miss you
I'm trying not to think about it
Trying doesn't work

Gifts

What you didn't know
Is that I had a gift for you waiting in my closet
What you didn't know
Was how much you had meant to me
What you didn't know
Is that I would have filled my closet with gifts for you
What you didn't know
Is how kind and sweet I would be
What you didn't know
Is how much love I had to bestow on you
What you didn't know
Is the freedom in my love's capacity
What you didn't know
Was my true nature in all the stuff that you didn't see
What you didn't know
When you said it wouldn't work for you
What you didn't know
When you said goodbye to me

<u>Love</u>

I'm going to pray for you
But not for me
For you
I pray that God speaks to your heart
That he softens the rough edges enough
For you to receive His great love
I pray that you will understand His amazing grace
That you allow that to sink in
And fill you in all the areas that you need it to
I pray that you let your spiritual knowledge expand
So that it speaks above your human nature
I pray that you will lay your burdens down
And accept the cross
I pray that God's love wraps you up like a blanket
Undeniable, unshakable, definitively
Amen.

Go Time

I'm not supposed to be thinking about you
Since letting you go

I'm not supposed to be dwelling in any sadness
Since letting you go

I'm not supposed to see your car at every stoplight
Or parked next to me at every place
It really is too much
As it's never you in the face

I'm doing my best to move on
Since letting you go

I'm supposed to feel free
Which I do on most days
I'm supposed to fight the thoughts of you that creep in
from time to time
I'm supposed to be healing and moving on
Which I am at most times

I'm supposed to let go
Since letting you go

And so
I'll stay the course and continue as so

Man

I don't want to be strong anymore
I want to be soft and let my fragility be exposed
I want a strong man to hold me
And tell me that everything is going to be ok
I want to believe him
I want to be the woman tucked under the wing
Protected as the sweetest and most precious little thing
Let me rest in my femininity
Wipe my weary tears away
Hold me close
Hold me tenderly
I need to recover the wind
That was taken, knocked out of me

Taking Thoughts Captive

Sadness go away
You don't belong here
Searching for my faith
In the mire of doubt
I know the promises
I know they are ahead of me
Barely keeping my head above the disappointing waves
Treading that dark water at night
The sharks would say, have fear
But the dawn is near
And despite the barren and abandoned surroundings of my heart
This is not end scene
This is the part where it seems all hope is lost, but alas,
I'm still breathing
Transition fades…
A bright future emerges
As all the pieces come together harmoniously
And so it is so, a re-write exposed
Heavy lungs nevermore
Exhale now for sure
Richness in love
Sadness a bore

<u>Open</u>

I'm not afraid of the hurt
But I still feel its intensity

I will not fear the rawness of love
For I still feel its intensity

Love seems to carry the risk of hurting
And hurt is tied to the ones we've loved

But I will not allow myself to be hardened by the hurt
I will not block the potential for greatest love

Loving Myself

Today is the last day that I let myself bleed for you
Sutures ready, time to cauterize this open wound
Won't come without a sting, a lingering burn, or without tears
A final cry into the night
A soul cry
The acceptance of a love lost without warning
I will always wonder why
I will always wonder how
How it could be that you couldn't see past your brokenness to find happiness with me
Stitches bear a temporary tear
Each one a fresh little wound of it's own
But without more pain, there can be no proper closure
Nice and neat, I weave this needle of healing
Careful to line up the jagged edges of disbelief, rejection, and scorn
My heart, a rose, would be incomplete without a stem of thorn
Another heart note to self
In the blanket of night
My constant companion
The time that I write
When I speak of the love that burst out my seams
It is love that makes me
That and my dreams
So farewell my dear one
May you find what you are looking for
To each his own
Or another time may be in store
But now I let go
And return to my task
Of loving myself enough to end this sadness
These stitches will fade
And my heart will show scars
Your memory sewn with me
Forever in me, my moon, my stars

Experience

I am very tired of having a sad heart
I want to write about living and loving happily

Kintsugi

To be loved by her
Is truly to be loved
For all that you are
From your potential to your broken places

She fears not the power of love
And you are lucky to receive it
A force of nature
Fierce and tender all together

To be loved by her
To be swept up in her grace
Is her favorite gift to give
It is free and flowing and never ending

Her heart is solid
Despite the wreckage some have made of it
She takes those pieces one by one
Forming mosaic love for everyone

The Call

I am human
It is only fair
To shine my love light
Wave it in the air

Sending the message
That I am ready
Despite the wind and rain
I'll hold it steady

Waiting for a signal
A sign from the other side
A love that will match me
Unwrap me and confide

Unafraid to be exposed
Opened to the extreme
Unashamed to stand alone
Yet wanting on a team

I will wait here for you
For the fog to fade away
Shine for me darling
Yellow, blue, or gray

We will be so lucky
For our light to come together
Come wind or sunshine
Love anchored in the weather

www.ingramcontent.com/pod-product-compliance
Lightning Source LLC
Chambersburg PA
CBHW050917160426
43194CB00011B/2449